Ice Age
SABERTOOTH

THE MOST FEROCIOUS CAT THAT EVER LIVED

By Barbara Hehner / Illustrations by Mark Hallett

Scientific consultation by Dr. Mark Engstrom and Dr. Kevin Seymour

A MADISON PRESS BOOK

produced for

CROWN PUBLISHERS ♔ NEW YORK

TRAPPED!

he powerful cat crouched in a clump of sage, the plants' fragrance masking his own musky scent. His haunches quivered as he studied the bison herd grazing nearby. It was spring, and there were many calves. Yet the cat hesitated. Although he was well armed with gigantic saberteeth, the adult bison were more than twice his size.

A calf ambled closer to the cat's hiding place. Suddenly, the young bison stumbled in a patch of fallen leaves. Struggling to rise but unable to get back on its feet, the calf cried out in distress. The huge cat broke cover and raced toward it.

The panicked bison herd ran off in confusion. Springing forward on powerful back legs, the cat pounced on the calf. With his deadly saberteeth, he delivered a quick killing bite and began to tear hungrily at his meal. Then he saw movement out of the corner of his eye: a pack of wolves was closing in.

The cat snarled and tried to turn toward the newcomers but found that he, too, was trapped. His paws were held fast in something dark and sticky. The more he struggled, the heavier his legs became. Several of the wolves, hoping to steal the cat's prey, instead found that they had joined him in a desperate battle to free themselves. Writhing in panic and howling in terror, the animals only succeeded in becoming more thoroughly mired in the black, gooey liquid. Overhead, a few enormous condors began to circle. They were looking for their next meal.

THE TREASURE OF
RANCHO LA BREA

The sabertooth cat and the wolves did not escape on that spring day some 20,000 years ago. They died in pools of thick asphalt that oozed naturally from the ground at a place now known as Rancho La Brea (Spanish for "tar ranch"), commonly called the La Brea tar pits.

Today the asphalt pools are in the middle of downtown Los Angeles. But in the time when sabertooths lived and hunted their prey, the area was a plain dotted with scrub growth and stands of pine and cypress trees.

A mastodon (top left), two Shasta ground sloths (middle right), and some flat-headed peccaries (bottom left and right) wander in what was once a forested area of Rancho La Brea. All are now extinct.

THE TAR PITS THAT AREN'T

The sticky black goo that trapped prehistoric animals at Rancho La Brea was actually asphalt, a naturally occurring substance, and not tar, which is made by humans. Asphalt is a type of crude oil formed deep below the surface of the earth. Through cracks caused by movements in the earth's crust, oil continues to seep to the surface today as it has done for thousands of years.

Asphalt does not collect in deep pits but in shallow pools. The ancient asphalt formed traps that held animals as though they were stuck to flypaper. Just a few inches could immobilize an animal as large as a mammoth.

Visitors to the George C. Page Museum of La Brea Discoveries in Los Angeles can view the fossils on display (above), watch bones being cleaned and repaired, and see a life-sized replica of a Columbian mammoth struggling to escape an asphalt pool.

This skeleton of a giant sloth (left) found at Rancho La Brea is just one of 59 different mammals discovered here since 1906.

A thin layer of dust, water, or leaves probably hid the treacherous sticky patches from the grazing animals that stumbled into them. Their struggles drew the predators, who then became trapped, too. As time went by, the bones of all these animals sank beneath the surface and were preserved in a thick coating of hardened asphalt.

Only a few animals were trapped each year. But over a long period of about 30,000 years, thousands of creatures — including mammoths, camels, horses, giant sloths, birds of prey, wolves, and big cats such as the sabertooth — died at Rancho La Brea. Since 1906, fossils of 59 kinds of mammals and over 135 kinds of birds have been uncovered, along with reptiles, plants, insects, and even snails. The most common large animal found at La Brea is an extinct wolf called the dire wolf. The next most common — bones from about 2,000 individuals have been discovered — is the sabertooth cat known to scientists as *Smilodon fatalis*.

SABERTOOTH CATS AND

ancho La Brea is a time capsule of the wildlife that lived in what is now Southern California during the last ice age. Not only was this an age of powerfully built cats, it was a time of enormous plant-eaters for them to prey on.

Biggest of all the La Brea plant-eaters were the Columbian mammoths, standing 13 feet (4 m) tall at the shoulder and wielding curved tusks up to 16 feet (5 m) long. Smaller and shaggier mastodons, another ancient type of elephant, grazed nearby. Migrating bison herds visited this region, some of them with menacing horns similar to

THEIR PREY: THE ANIMALS OF RANCHO LA BREA

those of today's long-horned cattle. The area was also home to wild horses, camels, deer, pronghorn antelope — and giant ground sloths. These bear-sized animals stood on their hind legs to strip the leaves off trees.

But the big cats did not have the banquet all to themselves. Dire wolves, larger and more ruggedly built than today's timber wolves, hunted in packs. Giant short-faced bears, which would have towered over today's largest grizzly bears, also prowled Rancho La Brea. Despite the bears' huge size, scientists are uncertain whether they were predators capable of running down prey or scavengers that let other animals do the hunting and then muscled in for a share of the kill.

The following animals are now extinct:

1) Dire wolf
2) Short-faced bear
3) American lion
4) Smilodon fatalis
5) Columbian mammoth
6) Western horse
7) Harlan's ground sloth
8) Yesterday's camel

THE ICE AGE

The cats that lived in North America three or four million years ago enjoyed a mild climate. The oceans around North America were much warmer than they are today, and trees grew well above the Arctic Circle. But over the next million years, temperatures gradually dropped and winters became longer, until much of the planet was in the grip of an ice age. It began about 1.7 million years ago and ended about 10,000 years ago. This time is also known as the Pleistocene Epoch. About 20,000 years ago, ice covered much of Europe, Asia, and North America. In North America, the ice reached as far south as present-day Missouri.

While no animals could live right on the ice, some of them lived on the windswept tundra nearby — including woolly mammoths and the rugged scimitar cats (another type of sabertooth) that preyed on them. Farther south, in the area of Rancho La Brea, the climate remained milder, although it was much cooler and wetter than it is today.

During this ice age, sea levels were much lower than they are now because so much water was frozen in the ice sheets. Siberia and Alaska were linked by a vast, grassy plain known as Beringia, and animals could migrate from one continent to the other on dry land. Human beings may have entered North America for the first time during the ice age, probably following herds of game animals. Scimitar cats and huge lions made the journey, too, while in North America, new forms of cat, including Smilodon, evolved.

WHAT CAUSES AN ICE AGE?

Though no one knows exactly what causes an ice age, scientists believe that a combination of factors might work together to bring about colder winters and cooler summers. Changes in the way the earth orbits around the sun, for example, could bring more sunlight to some parts of the planet and less to others. Shifts in the earth's atmosphere, such as a drop in the amount of carbon dioxide, might also cause temperatures to fall. As the continents moved and new mountain ranges were formed, wind and weather patterns could have altered, causing even more snow to fall. So much snow would have fallen that it didn't completely melt, even in summer. Over time, huge ice sheets, called glaciers, spread over the earth. The dazzling white ice reflected most of the sun's heat, bouncing the warming rays back into space.

FACE TO FACE WITH A VANISHED CAT

So what did Smilodon look like? Slightly larger than an African lion, but much heavier and more massively built, Smilodon weighed as much as 800 pounds (363 kg) and had a large head, powerful front legs, and a short tail. Its jaws opened to a gaping 95 degrees; by comparison, the widest yawn today's lions and tigers can manage is about 65 degrees. Smilodon needed to open wide to wield its most formidable weapons — a pair of curving, seven-inch (17-cm) long upper teeth with inner edges serrated like steak knives. They were as long and as sharp as the teeth of a *Tyrannosaurus rex*!

Because so many of their bones were preserved at Rancho La Brea, we know more about Smilodon than

about any other prehistoric cat. Still, only their bones have been found. We don't have a single tuft of fur, not even a whisker, to help us put flesh on those bones. Even though Smilodon died out just 10,000 years ago, well after human beings had invaded its territory, no ancient art shows this cat. Unlike mammoths — known not just from cave paintings but also from complete bodies found frozen in Siberia — we don't know exactly what saber-tooths looked like. Even so, paleontologists have been able to make many educated guesses about how these extinct cats looked and behaved. And studying modern cats is the place to start.

Many wild cats in the world today have striped or spotted fur. These broken patterns of light and dark help them lurk unseen in trees or behind bushes to ambush their prey. Scientists reason that because Smilodon also lived among trees and shrubs, it might have had a spotted coat — like today's leopards and jaguars.

Some scientists believe that sabertooth cats lived in groups. Today the African lion is the only big cat that lives in groups — called prides — and it is also the only cat with a mane. The mane identifies a mature male, both

SMILODON FATALIS

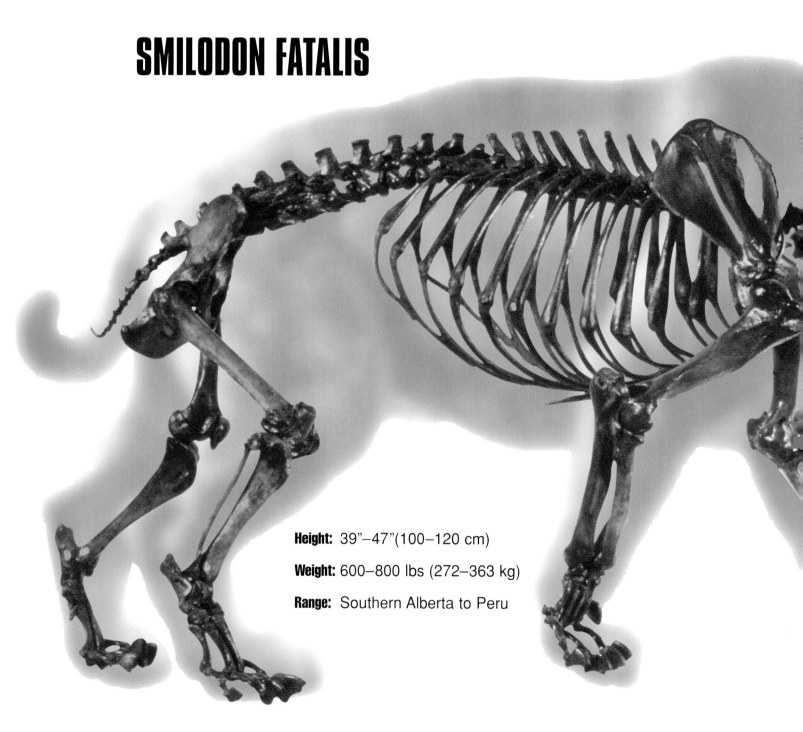

Height: 39"–47"(100–120 cm)

Weight: 600–800 lbs (272–363 kg)

Range: Southern Alberta to Peru

to other pride members and to lions from outside the group. So perhaps male Smilodon cats had manes, too.

Scientists also think that Smilodon had a stiff spray of whiskers on either side of its face. Whiskers, they reason, are so important to all living cats that prehistoric cats must have had them, too. A leopard, for instance, pulls its whiskers forward to touch its prey as it bites into its throat. These sensitive whiskers, connected to nerves in the leopard's face, help the cat place an accurate bite. In fact, scientists have discovered that Smilodon skulls have canals in them matching those in the skulls of modern cats. In living cats, these canals contain nerves for the face whiskers.

Smilodon bones also hint at the chilling sounds this long-vanished cat might have made. Small throat bones called hyoids are similar in shape in Smilodon to those found in today's lions. Did the roar of a sabertooth rumble like distant thunder and make herds of wild horses stampede in panic? Did the noise strike fear into the hearts of early Native Americans, armed only with spears and arrows?

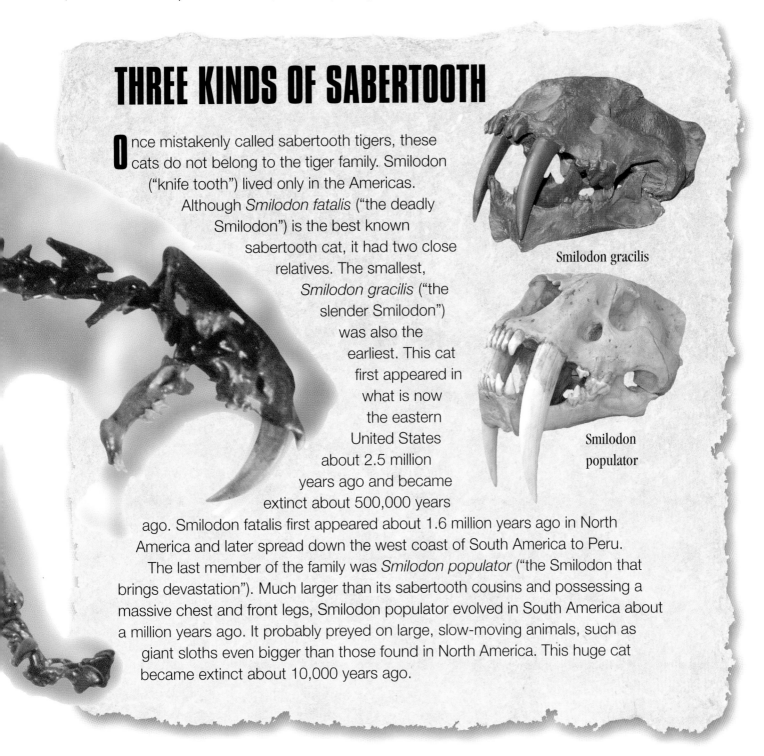

THREE KINDS OF SABERTOOTH

Once mistakenly called sabertooth tigers, these cats do not belong to the tiger family. Smilodon ("knife tooth") lived only in the Americas. Although *Smilodon fatalis* ("the deadly Smilodon") is the best known sabertooth cat, it had two close relatives. The smallest, *Smilodon gracilis* ("the slender Smilodon") was also the earliest. This cat first appeared in what is now the eastern United States about 2.5 million years ago and became extinct about 500,000 years ago. Smilodon fatalis first appeared about 1.6 million years ago in North America and later spread down the west coast of South America to Peru.

The last member of the family was *Smilodon populator* ("the Smilodon that brings devastation"). Much larger than its sabertooth cousins and possessing a massive chest and front legs, Smilodon populator evolved in South America about a million years ago. It probably preyed on large, slow-moving animals, such as giant sloths even bigger than those found in North America. This huge cat became extinct about 10,000 years ago.

Smilodon gracilis

Smilodon populator

KILLER TEETH

Although no cats today have saberteeth, these deadly weapons have made their appearance more than once in prehistoric animals. At the same time as the cat family tree was branching out, another group of carnivores developed that looked very much like sabertooth cats. But today most scientists consider them a separate group called the nimravids. One of the most impressive of these was the lion-sized *Barbourofelis*, which appeared in North America between 15 and 7 million years ago. This animal had retractable claws and 9-inch (23-cm) saberteeth, the longest ever seen. Unlike Smilodon, its saberteeth rested

BRINGING THE PAST TO LIFE

To picture what a sabertooth cat might have looked like, we rely on a process called restoration. A paleoartist — an illustrator who specializes in re-creating prehistoric animals — begins by carefully studying the bones of an extinct creature. Working with experts in animal motion, the artist tries to picture how the bones might have moved in the living animal. From marks and rough spots on the bones, the artist can tell where some of the muscles were located. Finally, by looking at the sabertooth's living relatives, such as lions and tigers, the artist gives everything a covering of fur, skin, and whiskers and brings Smilodon to life.

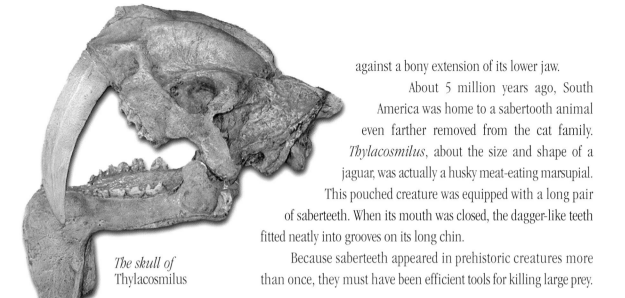

The skull of
Thylacosmilus

against a bony extension of its lower jaw.

About 5 million years ago, South America was home to a sabertooth animal even farther removed from the cat family. *Thylacosmilus*, about the size and shape of a jaguar, was actually a husky meat-eating marsupial. This pouched creature was equipped with a long pair of saberteeth. When its mouth was closed, the dagger-like teeth fitted neatly into grooves on its long chin.

Because saberteeth appeared in prehistoric creatures more than once, they must have been efficient tools for killing large prey.

A GOOD IDEA IS WORTH REPEATING

When scientists study the huge variety of animals that have lived on earth, they sometimes see the same physical feature occur again and again. For instance, in different parts of the world today, there are animals that specialize in eating ants, including the spiny anteater (*echidna*) of New Guinea and the scaly anteater (*pangolin*) of Africa and Asia. Although these animals are not at all related to each other, both have sharp claws to dig up ant nests, pointy snouts to poke around with, and long, sticky tongues to trap the ants before they can scurry away. This development of similar physical features in unrelated animals is called *evolutionary convergence*.

(Top) Spiny anteater, echidna. *(Above) Scaly anteater,* pangolin.

HOW DID THE SABERTOOTH ATTACK ITS PREY?

Because Smilodon was so heavy and because its legs were relatively short, scientists think it could not have chased and overtaken prey in open country as a cheetah does. The sabertooth also lacked a long tail, which cats use for balance and for making sudden changes in direction as they run. Whether in groups or by itself, Smilodon probably hid and ambushed its prey. Still, this hefty cat could probably sprint for a short distance at about 30 miles (48 km) per hour, the speed of a medium-sized bear. It then used its powerful front legs and strong jaw and neck muscles to seize and overpower its prey. But what did it do next?

Some living cats — including cheetahs and domestic cats — kill their prey with a bite to the back of the neck. But sabertooth cats probably did not kill this way. While their long saberteeth looked menacing, they could snap off easily if they hit solid bone. Many La Brea cats suffered broken jaws and shoulder bones, probably fractured by a well-aimed hoof. Others have been found with chipped or broken saberteeth, perhaps damaged by their twisting and thrashing prey.

(Left) From its hiding place among the grasses, a sabertooth cat gets ready to pounce. Its prey, an American elk, grazes unsuspectingly.

Surprise Attack

1) *Breaking from its cover, the sabertooth would spring forward,* **2)** *then sprint for a short distance before* **3)** *using its powerful front legs and claws to bring down the elk.*

3

THE PERFECT HUNTING MACHINE

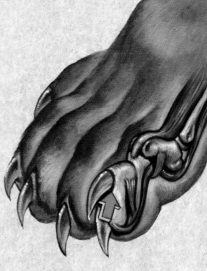

Cats have been called "the perfect hunting machine." From the beginning, all cats have been carnivores, or meat-eaters. Most of them have hunted by themselves, leaping from cover to ambush their prey. They hold and kill their victims with strong front limbs and sharp claws and teeth. When they are not using their claws, cats retract them (pull them back into their paws) so that they remain sharp (top).

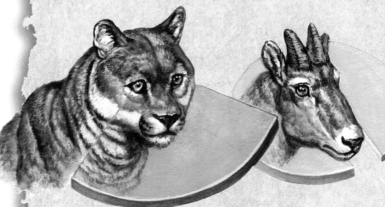

All cats have keen eyesight. Their eyes have always faced forward (above left), rather than to the side as they do in many plant-eating animals (above right). This creates an overlap in what they can see with their left and right eyes. The overlap is greater in cats than in most other meat-eating mammals, and it gives them excellent depth perception. This is the ability to judge how far away something is, a vital tool for a pouncing cat.

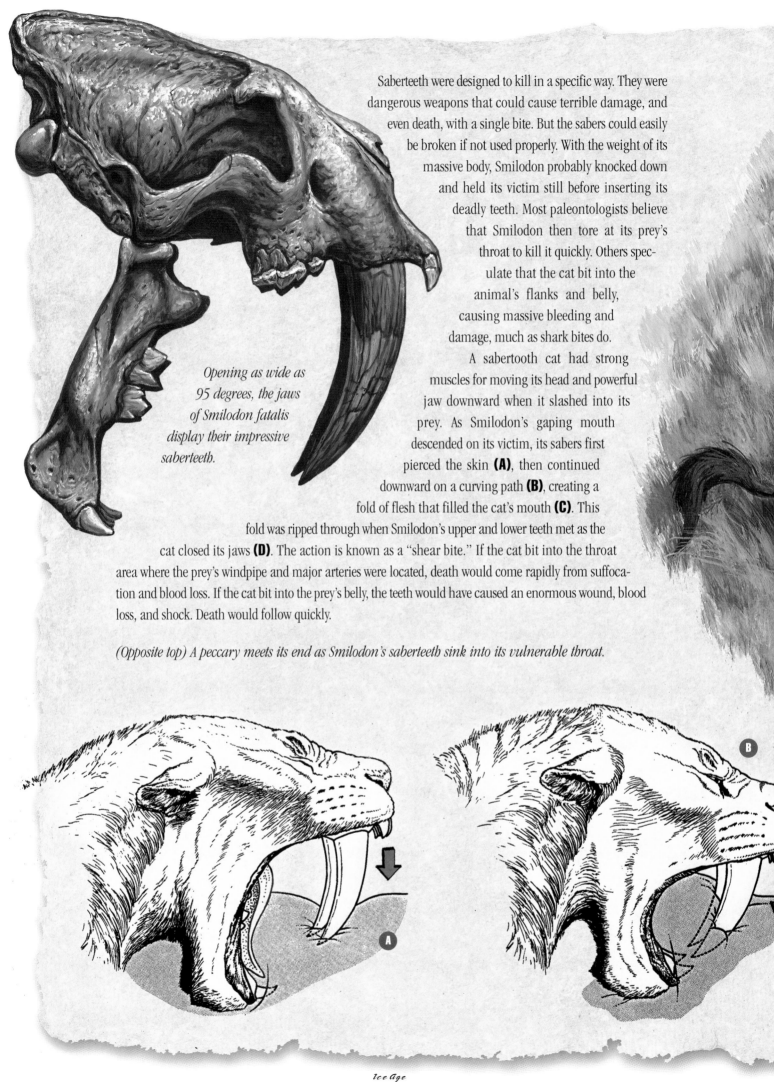

Saberteeth were designed to kill in a specific way. They were dangerous weapons that could cause terrible damage, and even death, with a single bite. But the sabers could easily be broken if not used properly. With the weight of its massive body, Smilodon probably knocked down and held its victim still before inserting its deadly teeth. Most paleontologists believe that Smilodon then tore at its prey's throat to kill it quickly. Others speculate that the cat bit into the animal's flanks and belly, causing massive bleeding and damage, much as shark bites do.

A sabertooth cat had strong muscles for moving its head and powerful jaw downward when it slashed into its prey. As Smilodon's gaping mouth descended on its victim, its sabers first pierced the skin **(A)**, then continued downward on a curving path **(B)**, creating a fold of flesh that filled the cat's mouth **(C)**. This fold was ripped through when Smilodon's upper and lower teeth met as the cat closed its jaws **(D)**. The action is known as a "shear bite." If the cat bit into the throat area where the prey's windpipe and major arteries were located, death would come rapidly from suffocation and blood loss. If the cat bit into the prey's belly, the teeth would have caused an enormous wound, blood loss, and shock. Death would follow quickly.

(Opposite top) A peccary meets its end as Smilodon's saberteeth sink into its vulnerable throat.

Opening as wide as 95 degrees, the jaws of Smilodon fatalis display their impressive saberteeth.

Did the sabertooth cat live and hunt alone, or did it live with others of its kind? Among the Smilodon skeletons discovered at Rancho La Brea, a number were old and battle-scarred. One cat had such damaged hip and leg bones that it could barely have dragged itself along the ground. It could not possibly have hunted. Yet it survived, and its broken bones mended before it was trapped in the sticky asphalt. To some paleontologists, healed injuries such as these suggest that Smilodon might have lived in groups the way African lions do. They argue that stronger cats must have shared their food with the weaker ones.

A pride of lions may have as many as 40 members. Most of them are related females, with their young. The adult males have joined the group from other prides in which they were raised. Often, male lions must drive off their rivals before they can earn a place in a new pride and the right to a mate. Did Smilodon live like this, too? We know that the adult cats fought with each other from time to time: some Smilodon bones show holes inflicted by other sabertooth cats. Perhaps some of the

Two sabertooth cats attack a giant sloth.

injuries happened when rival males battled one another over a kill, over territory, or over control of a pack.

Female lions do most of the hunting for the pride. Since their bodies are too bulky for long chases, the lionesses use strategy and cooperation to capture their prey. Several of them drive an animal, such as an antelope, toward other cats lying in wait. Then the lionesses attack together to bring the antelope down. Because of the massive size of some of its prehistoric prey, Smilodon may have had to hunt in groups, too.

When researchers counted the bones discovered at Rancho La Brea, they found that for each large plant-eater trapped in the asphalt, five to ten saber-tooth cats were trapped as well. It is likely that even more were caught in the sticky pits but managed to save themselves. Some scientists say that this puts so many Smilodons in one place at one time that there is only one explanation: they must have hunted in packs.

But other scientists disagree. Because the lion is the only cat that has evolved pride behavior, they believe it is highly unusual for a cat species to act this way. They do not think Smilodon lived and hunted in groups. Veterinary evidence shows that injured cats have an unusual ability to heal rapidly, even without food. As long as they can reach water, cats can survive an injury while fasting through it. The repair mechanisms of their bodies continue to function even if they don't eat. Perhaps the healed injuries of the sabertooth cats at Rancho La Brea just indicate that the animals survived by fasting, only to be caught in the asphalt later while trying to eat other creatures trapped there.

Still locked together after thousands of years, the fang of one sabertooth cat remains embedded in the fractured shoulder blade of another.

STARTING FROM SCRATCH

All the prehistoric cats like Smilodon and all the cats in the world today, from lions to domestic cats, probably descend from a compact animal called *Proailurus*. Proailurus lived in Europe about 30 million years ago and died out approximately 20 million years ago. If you could magically transport a Proailurus forward in time to your own backyard, you would have no trouble recognizing it. Glaring down at you from your backyard tree, with its large eyes, long tail, and sharp teeth and claws, Proailurus could not be mistaken for anything but a cat. In fact, it was only a little larger than a big tabby cat, weighing about 20 pounds (9 kg), and probably spent much of its life in trees.

Proailurus
30–20 million years ago

The next cat clawing its way along the family tree is known as *Pseudaelurus*. Appearing about 20 million years ago, Pseudaelurus was also an agile climber. Bones of these cats have been found in several places in Europe and also in North America. Pseudaelurus was a much bigger cat than Proailurus, and it had become the size of a cougar by the time it died out about 10 million years ago. By then, the cat family was branching in several directions.

Smilodon was not the first cat to have deadly saberteeth. About 13 million years ago and long before Smilodon first appeared, a different kind of sabertooth cat called *Machairodus* existed. This huge cat, as big as a lion, was also a fierce meat-eater and lived in Europe, Asia, Africa, and North America. It died out about 2 million years ago. In the time of Machairodus, none of the "big cats" we know today had yet appeared in the world.

The bones of leopard-sized *Dinofelis*, which appeared about 5 million years ago, have also been found in Europe, Asia, Africa, and North America. This cat is called a "false sabertooth" because its teeth were midway between long, flat saberteeth and the cone-shaped teeth of lions and other cats alive today. In South Africa, its bones have been found with those of the baboons it killed. Baboons are strong and aggressive primates that live in communities. If Dinofelis was powerful enough to kill them, it may also have attacked some of our earliest human ancestors more than 2 million years ago.

By the time Dinofelis died out about 1.5 million years ago, the world was a different place, and the cat family had been transformed. The ice age — the time of mammoths and mastodons, huge deer and bison, and woolly rhinoceroses — had arrived. The cats that preyed on these giants were the most powerful the world has ever seen.

WHY IS THE FAMILY TREE SO HARD TO DRAW?

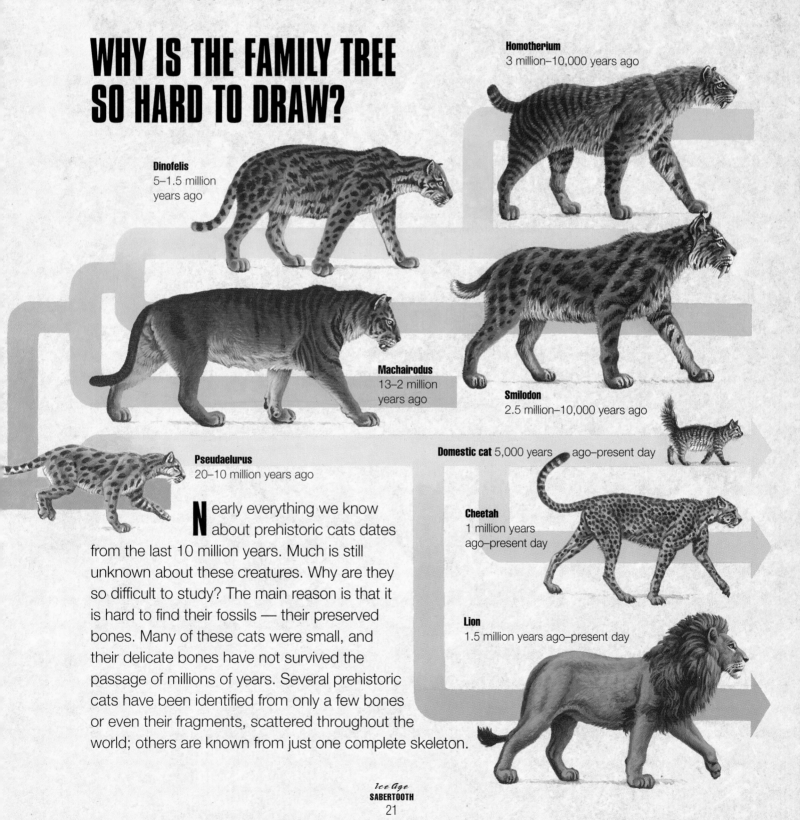

Homotherium
3 million–10,000 years ago

Dinofelis
5–1.5 million years ago

Machairodus
13–2 million years ago

Smilodon
2.5 million–10,000 years ago

Pseudaelurus
20–10 million years ago

Domestic cat 5,000 years ago–present day

Cheetah
1 million years ago–present day

Lion
1.5 million years ago–present day

Nearly everything we know about prehistoric cats dates from the last 10 million years. Much is still unknown about these creatures. Why are they so difficult to study? The main reason is that it is hard to find their fossils — their preserved bones. Many of these cats were small, and their delicate bones have not survived the passage of millions of years. Several prehistoric cats have been identified from only a few bones or even their fragments, scattered throughout the world; others are known from just one complete skeleton.

ICE AGE CATS OF NORTH AMERICA

Scientists agree that Smilodon was a New World cat. But it had company in North America: several other large cats likely crossed from Asia to Alaska across the windswept plains of Beringia.

Homotherium serum is also known as the scimitar cat. Its saberteeth were shorter than those of Smilodon but were serrated on both sides. Homotherium was about the height of a modern lion. Unlike the stocky Smilodon, the scimitar cat was built to run — perhaps as fast as 60 miles (96 km) per hour. Although it may have been outnumbered by Smilodon, Homotherium had a larger range, from Texas all the way up to Alaska and the Yukon. At the Friesenhahn Cave in Texas, paleontologists have uncovered a Homotherium den, with the remains of 13 cubs and 20 adult cats. Also in the cave are the bones of hundreds of young mammoths, suggesting that groups of these scimitar cats hunted them together.

Along with lion-sized cats, North America was once home to an actual lion: *Panthera atrox*. Unlike the sabertooth and scimitar cats, the American lion was a close relative of the African lion. The bones of

A group of scimitar cats, with mammoth bones scattered around them, take shelter in the Friesenhahn Cave in Texas.

more than 80 lions have been found at Rancho La Brea, so their body structure is well known. They were the biggest North American cats of their day, with males weighing as much as half a ton (450 kg). They ranged all the way from Alaska and the Yukon to central Mexico. The frozen carcass of a bison, killed 36,000 years ago and found near Fairbanks, Alaska, in 1979, showed the marks of a lion attack.

Until very recently, paleontologists believed there were only two sabertooth cats in ice age North America: Smilodon and Homotherium. But then a third was discovered! The cat's bones were found in Florida in 1981, but it was only in 1999 that Larry Dean Martin, a paleontologist at the University of Kansas, had the chance to study them. He was astounded by what he saw — a cat that probably weighed about 450 pounds (203 kg), with the hefty build of Smilodon but the shorter, broader saberteeth of Homotherium. For now, the mystery cat has been given the name *Xenosmilus* ("strange tooth").

The reconstructed skull of Xenosmilus *displays its formidable set of teeth.*

A snarling clouded leopard offers a glimpse of its lengthy canine teeth.

A MODERN SABERTOOTH?

Will the world ever see the sabertooth cat return? In the rainforests of Southeast Asia lives a mysterious and seldom-seen cat called the clouded leopard. It weighs about 50 pounds (23 kg), and has a long body and short, powerful legs. Its beautiful coat, with large rosettes of black and gray on a tawny background, camouflages the cat as it hides high in tree branches, silent and deadly, waiting for its prey to pass. Then it leaps down from a branch to overpower wild boar and deer. These are large animals for a cat that is smaller than a golden retriever to tackle, but the clouded leopard is well armed. It has the largest canines (the pointed fangs on either side of the mouth) relative to its body size, of any living cat — about two and a half inches (over 6 cm) long. Could the clouded leopard ever become a new sabertooth cat? Given long enough, perhaps it could, but the clouded leopard may be running out of time in the wild. Human beings are rapidly destroying its rainforest habitat.

WHAT KILLED THE SABERTOOTH CATS?

About 10,000 years ago, Smilodon, along with scimitar cats and lions, became extinct in North America. Around the same time, two-thirds of the other large mammals — including mammoths, mastodons, giant sloths, camels, and dire wolves — died out. Large mammals also became extinct in South America, northern Europe, and Asia, as did many large marsupials of Australia. What defeated these rugged animals? They had survived the severe conditions of the ice age only to succumb when the world's climates became milder. Were human beings to blame?

We know that early Native Americans first arrived in North America a few thousand years before the sabertooths and other large cats disappeared. But their small bands were widely scattered across the continent. They were armed only with spears and arrows, and the cats had formidable weapons in their teeth and claws. Did cats kill human beings? Did human beings kill cats? It's logical to think that both events occurred, but proof is hard to find. No ancient human bones have been discovered that show signs of a sabertooth attack. American lion bones have been found at one native archaeological site in Idaho, suggesting that human beings may have hunted them, but the evidence is unclear.

Most scientists agree that human beings did not wipe out the cats by attacking them directly. But humans might have overhunted the huge animals the cats preyed on. Then the cats might have died out because their food source had vanished.

But other scientists are not convinced that human beings caused any of the extinctions at the end of the ice age. They argue that large mammals and humans lived together in Europe and Asia for thousands of years before the animals died out. Furthermore, in Africa, both large plant-eaters and the big cats that preyed on them survived into modern times, despite being hunted. These scientists have suggested instead that, as the temperature and rainfall changed, the vegetation that provided cover for sabertooth cats to ambush their prey died. The food plants the herbivores depended on may have also disappeared. If the plant-eaters died of starvation, then the meat-eaters would soon have followed them. Saberteeth would be of no use if the cats had nothing large enough to prey on.

Prehistoric hunters drive a group of now-extinct western horses down a cliff as a lone sabertooth watches from above.

Lion

Tiger

● **PANTHERA**

Leopard

Jaguar

THREATENED ON ALL SIDES

There are about 37 cat species in the world today. Traditionally, scientists have organized them into two or three groups. The first group, *Panthera*, includes four big cats: lions, tigers, leopards, and jaguars. The Asian tiger is the heavyweight of this group, with males sometimes weighing more than 600 pounds (270 kg). The jaguar is the only Panthera cat found outside Asia and Africa — in Central and South America. All these cats have voice boxes that can produce thunderous roars.

The African cheetah is such a unique cat that it is sometimes placed in a group by itself: *Acinonyx*. Cheetahs are medium-sized cats, weighing about 125 pounds (50 kg), with small dome-shaped heads, slim, light bones, and

● **ACINONYX** *Cheetah*

Cougar   ● **FELIS**   *Rusty Spotted Cat*

long legs. They are the world's fastest land animals, able to go from a standstill to 45 miles (72 km) per hour in 2.5 seconds. They hunt in open country, chasing down gazelles and other fleet-footed prey.

The last traditional cat group, *Felis*, includes all the remaining species. The domestic cat, known as *Felis catus*, is in this group. Wild Felis cats, found all over the world, are usually striped or spotted and hunt rodents, birds, and other small prey. Most weigh 30 pounds (14 kg) or less, and the smallest, the rusty spotted cat of India and Sri Lanka, weighs only three pounds (1.3 kg). The only truly large cat of this group is the cougar, which can weigh up to 200 pounds (90 kg). Felis cats growl, meow, purr, and hiss, but they cannot roar.

In recent years, scientists have been studying the genetic code — the chemical instructions in every body cell of an animal that guide its growth and appearance — of living cats. They have been able to make more accurate groupings of cats, based on which ones are most similar in their genetic makeup. The four big cats are still grouped together. But there have been surprises. It turns out, for example, that cheetahs are most closely related to cougars.

Nearly all of the bigger cats are endangered, as well as many of the smaller ones. This time there is no doubt that human beings are to blame. Leopards have been overhunted for their beautiful spotted coats, and tigers for traditional medicines made from their organs. All cats need hunting territories, and the forests and grasslands where they once stalked their prey are disappearing all over the world. A growing human population is taking over more and more land for farms, roads, and cities, squeezing the cats out.

THE WORLD'S MOST SUCCESSFUL CAT

The cat pounces, digging in with its sharp claws and biting the neck of its prey. The mouse doesn't stand a chance. A few stitches pop open and catnip sprays across the carpet.

Meet the world's most successful cat — Felis catus, the domestic cat. Its ancestors were small, tabby-striped wild cats that were once widespread in Europe, Asia, and Africa. About 5,000 years ago, around the time that human beings were first starting to farm and settle in villages, cats struck a bargain with them: you take care of me, and I will keep the vermin out of your fields and granaries. Today, in the United States alone, 66 million cats are kept as house pets. Most of these cats do not have to keep their original bargain. For their admirers, it is enough that they are purring, graceful companions. But the fascination of domestic cats is that they never seem completely tame.

Every cat alive today — from lions and tigers to house pets — is an equally distant relative of the long-extinct sabertooth. To bring Smilodon back to life, if only in your imagination, just watch a house cat. It crouches, haunches wriggling with tension, tail switching, its eyes focused only on its prey. And at exactly the right moment, it leaps.

In a modern game of cat and mouse, a tabby toys with its electronic prey.

GLOSSARY

carnivore: An animal that eats the flesh of other animals.

herbivore: An animal that eats only plant material.

mammal: Warm-blooded animals with fur or hair that nourish their young with milk.

marsupial: Animals whose young are born very early and continue to develop in a protected area of the mother's belly, often inside a flap of skin or pouch.

peccary: A pig-like animal with coarse hair and cloven feet. Some types are now extinct.

Pleistocene Epoch: The period from approximately 1.7 million to 10,000 years ago, marked by great changes in temperature and sheets of ice advancing and retreating across the earth.

predator: A creature that hunts and kills other animals for food.

primate: A member of the mammal order that includes monkeys, apes, and human beings.

sage: An aromatic herb that grows wild in many parts of the world.

species: A single kind of plant or animal.

vermin: Small animals that cause damage to crops and are difficult to control.

RECOMMENDED FURTHER READING

For young readers:

Death Trap: The Story of the La Brea Tar Pits
by Sharon Elaine Thompson, Lerner Publications
● A thorough look at the geologic history of Rancho La Brea and the many fossils discovered there.

For older readers:

The Big Cats and Their Fossil Relatives
by Alan Turner, illustrations by Mauricio Antón,
Columbia University Press
● This adult-level scholarly book is noteworthy for its detailed information and for the beautifully rendered drawings of paleoartist Mauricio Antón.

WEB SITES

www.tarpits.org
The informative web site of the George C. Page Museum of La Brea Discoveries explains the formation of the asphalt traps and looks at the many fossils found there.

dsc.discovery.com/stories/nature/sabretooth/sabretooth.html
The Discovery Channel's web site includes a video demonstration of a sabertooth cat hunting, sabertooth trivia, and the chance to build your own supercat.

PICTURE CREDITS

All illustrations are by Mark Hallett unless otherwise stated.

5: (Top) Joel W. Rogers, CORBIS/Magma; (left) Ed Ikuta, courtesy of the George C. Page Museum

8: Map by Jack McMaster

10–11: Illustration by John C. Dawson, courtesy of the George C. Page Museum; skeleton, courtesy of the George C. Page Museum; (top right) Jerry Stark, courtesy of the University of Florida; (bottom right) Jerry Stark, B.I.O.P.S.I.

13: (Top) Jerry Stark, courtesy of Antiquarian Fossils Inc./

Museo de la Plata, Argentina; (middle) Pavel German, NHPA; (bottom) Daniel Heuclin, NHPA

20: James L. Amos, CORBIS/Magma

21: Illustration by Alan Barnard

24: Jerry Stark, B.I.O.P.S.I.

25: Andy Rouse, NHPA

28: (Top left) Anne and Steve Toon, NHPA; (top right) James Warwick, NHPA; (bottom left) Daryl Balfour, NHPA; (bottom right) Martin Harvey, NHPA

29: (Top) Martin Harvey, NHPA; (bottom left) Rebecca Grambo, Firstlight.ca; (bottom right) James L. Amos, CORBIS/Magma